TO:

_____

FROM:

_____

*Thanks for being such
a blessing to me!*

You're a Blessing to Me
© 2002 by The Zondervan Corporation

ISBN: 0-310-80582-1

Requests for information should be addressed to:
    Inspirio, The gift group of Zondervan
    Grand Rapids, Michigan 49530
    http://www.inspiriogifts.com

Compiler: Molly C. Detweiler
Design: Mark Veldheer

Printed in China
04 05 06/HK/ 4 3 2 1

YOU'RE A BLESSING TO ME

inspirio™

For listening to me with
a sympathetic ear
For bringing me little gifts
just to bring me cheer
For always having a smile
ready to brighten my day
I want to say you're a
blessing to me
in so very many ways!

The person who sows
seeds of kindness
enjoys a perpetual harvest.

Author Unknown

A kind heart is a fountain
of gladness, making
everything around it
fresh with smiles.

Washington Irving

Drop a word of cheer and kindness:
Just a flash and it is gone;
But there's half–a–hundred ripples
Circling on and on,
Bearing hope and joy and comfort on
Each splashing, dashing wave.
Till you wouldn't believe the volume
Of the one kind word you gave.

James W. Foley

I thank my God every time I remember
you. In all my prayers for all of you, I
always pray with joy.

Philippians 1:3–4

"You are precious and
    honored in my sight,
and...I love you,"
  says the LORD.

Isaiah 43:4

We can consider ourselves a
Loved Person, not because of our
circumstances or situations but
simply because God loves us
perfectly, totally, and eternally.

Marie Chapian

You have been God's way of cheering me up so many times.

Kind words can be short and easy to speak, but their echoes are truly endless.

Mother Teresa

An anxious heart weighs a man down,
but a kind word cheers him up.

Proverbs 12:25

One kind word can warm three winter months.

Ancient Proverb

If I can put one touch
of a rosy sunset into
the life of any man or
woman, I shall feel that I
have worked with God.

John MacDonald

You've warmed my heart
with your kind words—
thank you so much.

Patience is a virtue,
virtue is a grace.
Both put together,
make a pretty face.

Anonymous

*Your patience and grace shine
to everyone around you.*

*When I count my blessings
you are at the top of the list!*

Count your blessings,
Name them one by one,
Count your blessings,
See what God has done!
Count your blessings
Name them one by one
And it will surprise you
What the Lord has done!

Johnson Oatman Jr.

Those who bring sunshine
to the lives of others cannot
keep it from themselves.

I hope that you feel the
warmth of the sunshine
that you bring to others!

Grace and peace to you from God our Father and from the Lord Jesus Christ.

Romans 1:7

*Love is patient, love is kind.
It does not envy, it does not boast,
it is not proud. It is not rude, it is
not self-seeking, it is not easily
angered, it keeps no record of
wrongs. Love does not delight in
evil but rejoices with the truth.
It always protects, always trusts,
always hopes, always perseveres.
Love never fails.*

1 Corinthians 13:4–8

A happy heart makes the face cheerful.

Proverbs 15:13

Life is full of ups and downs
Everybody knows
But when you smile
Instead of frown
Your heart soon overflows!

A smile is a curve that sets things straight.

The LORD your God is with you,
  he is mighty to save.
He will take great delight in you,
  he will quiet you with his love,
  he will rejoice over you with
    singing.

Zephaniah 3:17

Encouragement is the oxygen of the soul.

Author Unknown

The really great person is the person who makes every person feel great.

G. K. Chesterton

Your love has given me great joy and encouragement.

Philemon 1:7

Encouragement costs nothing to give but is priceless to receive.

Author Unknown

Dare to be happy—
don't shy away,
Reach out and capture
the joy of today!

Dare to be happy,
don't be afraid—
This is the day which
the Lord has made!

Helen Lowrie Marshal

The world is round and the place which may seem like the end may also be only the beginning.

Author Unknown

Let the morning bring me word of
     your unfailing love, O LORD,
for I have put my trust in you.
Show me the way I should go,
    for to you I lift up my soul.

Psalm 143:8

Faith is the wire that connects you to grace, and over which grace comes streaming from God.

Anonymous

Isn't it comforting to know that God
is watching over us with his love?

Doris Rikkers

Faith is being sure of what we
hope for and certain of what
we do not see.

Hebrews 11:1

The LORD will keep you from all harm—
he will watch over your life;
the LORD will watch over your coming
and going
both now and forevermore.

Psalm 121:7–8

Many women do noble things,
but you surpass them all.
Charm is deceptive,
and beauty is fleeting;
but a woman who fears the
LORD is to be praised.
Give her the reward she
has earned.

Proverbs 31:29–31

May you be blessed by the LORD,
  the Maker of heaven and earth.

Psalm 115:15

The happiest business in all the
  world is that of making friends.
And no investment on the street pays
  larger dividends,
For life is more than stocks and bonds,
And love than rate percent,
And he who gives in friendship's name
Shall reap what he has spent.

Anonymous

BLESSINGS FOR YOU

I pray that out of God's glorious riches he may strengthen you with power through his Spirit in your inner being.

Ephesians 3:16

Dear friend, I pray that you may enjoy good health and that all may go well with you, even as your soul is getting along well.

3 John 1:2

May the LORD repay you for what you have done. May you be richly rewarded by the LORD.

Ruth 2:12

The highest form of
wisdom is kindness.

Linda Berman

*The wisdom that comes from
heaven is first of all pure; then
peace-loving, considerate,
submissive, full of mercy and good
fruit, impartial and sincere.*

James 3:17

The tongue of the wise
brings healing.

Proverbs 12:18

God who is love simply cannot help but shed blessing upon blessing upon us. We do not need to beg, for he simply cannot help it!

We know and rely on the love God has for us. God is love. Whoever lives in love lives in God, and God in him.

1 John 4:16

Follow the way of love.

1 Corinthians 14:1

Love is a gift sent
from on high
To unite souls as one
And make sorrows fly.
Hold dear as a diamond
This gift from above;
To make life worth living
Just follow God's love.

It's only with the heart that one can see clearly. The most important things are invisible to the eyes.

Antoine De Saint-Exupery

Only the heart knows how to find what is precious.

Fyodor Dostoyevsky

Blessed are the pure in heart, for they will see God.

Matthew 5:8

I'd like to do the big things
    and the splendid things for you,
To brush the gray from out of
        your skies
    and leave them only blue
I'd like to say the kindly things
    I so oft have heard,
And feel that I could rouse your
        soul
    the way that mind you've stirred.

Edgar A. Guest

I believe that God brings us many precious gifts during our lives—spectacular sunsets, good food, the warmth of the sunshine, and the refreshment of cool rains. But even with all those great gifts, and many more besides, he didn't stop there. He gave us people, people like you, who bless our lives with kindness.

If I could reach up and hold a star
for every time you've made me
smile, the entire evening sky
would be in the palm of my hand.

Author Unknown

*Every good and perfect gift is from
above, coming down from the Father
of the heavenly lights, who does not
change like shifting shadows.*

James 1:17

I never came to you and went away
without some new enrichment of the
heart; more faith and less of doubt.

Grace Noll Crowell

THANK YOU

You entered my life in a casual way,
And saw at a glance what I needed;
There were others who passed me or
    met me each day,
But never a one of them heeded.
Perhaps you were thinking of other
    folks more,
Or chance simply seemed to decree it;
I know there were many such chances
    before,
But the others—well, they didn't see it.

You said just the thing that I wished
  you would say,
And you made me believe that you
  meant it;
I held up my head, renewed much
  that day,
And resolved you should never
  regret it.
There are times when encouragement
  means such a lot,
And a word is enough to convey it;
There were others who could have,
  as easy as not—
But, just the same they didn't say it.

Grace Stricker Dawson

May there always be work for
　your hands to do,
May your purse always hold a
　coin or two.
May the sun always shine warm
　on your windowpane,
May a rainbow be certain to
　follow each rain.
May the hand of a friend always
　be near you,
And may God fill your heart
　with gladness to cheer you.

Irish Blessing

*Pleasant words are a honeycomb,
　sweet to the soul and healing
　　to the bones.*

Proverbs 16:24

A little word of kindness
spoken,
A motion or a tear,
Has often healed the heart
That's broken,
And made a friend sincere.

Daniel Clement Colesworthy

To the world you might
be just one person, but
to one person you might
just be the world.

Author Unknown

Your love has helped me handle
    the little ups and downs of life.
The moments that are tearful
    and full of lonely strife.
And then there are the moments
    full of cheerfulness and glee;
I'm so glad your heart is furnished
    with a little place for me.

Doris Rikkers

BLESSINGS FOR YOU

May your home always be too small to hold all your friends.

May the most you wish for be the least you get.

May your day be filled with
    blessings
Like the sun that lights the sky,
And may you always have the
    courage
To spread your wings and fly!

May God Almighty
bless you.

Genesis 28:3

You are encouraging
when I am discouraged;
Understanding when
I feel misunderstood;
Comforting when
I am uncomfortable.

Give, and it will given to you.
A good measure, pressed down,
shaken together and running over,
will be poured into your lap.

Luke 6:38

The LORD bless you
and keep you;
the LORD make his face shine
upon you
and be gracious to you;
the LORD turn his face toward you
and give you peace.

Numbers 6:24–26

THROUGH THE YEAR

God be with you in the Springtime
When the violets unfold,
And the buttercups and cowslips
Fill the fields with yellow gold.

God be with you in the Summer,
When the sweet June roses blow,
When the bobolinks are laughing
And the brooks with music flow.

God be with you in the Autumn,
When the birds and flowers have fled,
And along the woodland pathways
Leaves are falling, gold and red.

God be with you in the Winter,
When the snow lies deep and white,
When the sleeping fields are silent
And the stars gleam cold and bright.

Julian S. Cutler

Beauty is God's handwriting. Welcome it in every fair face, every fair day, every fair flower.

Charles Kingsley

The unfading beauty of a gentle and quiet spirit... is of great worth in God's sight.

1 Peter 3:4

There shall be showers of blessing, This is the promise of love. There shall be seasons refreshing, Sent from the Savior above.

Daniel W. Whittle

God has made everything
beautiful in its time.

Ecclesiastes 3:11

"I will send down showers
in season; there will
be showers of blessing,"
says the LORD.

Ezekiel 34:26

Oh the comfort—the inexpressible comfort of
feeling safe with a person,
Having neither to weigh
thoughts,
Nor measure words—but
pouring them
All right out—just as they are—
Chaff and grain together—
Certain that a faithful hand will
Take and sift them—
Keep what is worth keeping—
And with a breath of kindness
Blow the rest away.

Dinah Maria Mulock Craik

No gift is small when God accepts it.

Teresa of Avila

Your talent is God's gift to you. What you do with it is your gift back to God.

Leo Buscaglia

We have different gifts, according to the grace given us.

Romans 12:6

The best and most beautiful
things in the world cannot be
seen or even touched—they
must be felt with the heart.

Helen Keller

I will always have hope;
I will praise you more
and more, LORD.

Psalm 71:14

Faith makes all things possible.
Love makes all things easy.
Hope makes all things work.

The lovely memories
That God has given me
Help me to remember
That there are more to be.

Molly Detweiler

Hope is a thing with feathers—
That perches in the soul—
And sings the tune
Without the words—
And never stops—at all.

Emily Dickinson

If we sit down at set of sun
And count the acts that we have done,
And, counting, find
One self-denying act, one word
That eased the heart of him who heard
One glance most kind
That fell like sunshine where it went
Then we may count that day well spent.

Author Unknown

For the beauty of each hour,
Of the day and of the night,
Hill and dale, and tree and flower,
Sun and moon, and stars of light,
Lord of all, to Thee we raise,
This, our hymn of grateful praise.

Folliot S. Pierpoint

*How many are your works, O LORD!
In wisdom you made them all;
The earth is full of your creatures.*

Psalm 104:24

May the road rise to meet you.

May the wind be always

at your back.

May the sun shine warm

upon your face.

And the rain fall soft

upon your fields.

And until we meet again

May God hold you in

the palm of His hand.

Irish Blessing